BUILDING BLOCKS for BETTER FAMILIES

by Marilyn Hickey

Marilyn
Hickey
Ministries
P.O. Box 17340
Denver, CO 80217

Building Blocks for Better Families

CONTENTS

Introduction

The most precious thing you have is your family. Nothing touches you more than your children. There is nothing quite like seeing your child moved on by God. That's not surprising when we remember how much Jesus esteemed children:

"But Jesus said, 'Suffer little children, and forbid them not, to come unto me: for of such is the kingdom of heaven'" (Matthew 19:14).

He loved children! The Bible says children are a rich gift, an inheritance.

Parenting is the most rewarding job any of us will ever do! It is the most difficult, and the most frustrating. That is why God gave us so many "parenting tips" in the Bible. In this book, we are going to look at God's instructions for parents, and at God's hope and help for parents.

Do you know any perfect parents? Do you know any perfect children? Well, there may be some people who *say* they are perfect parents, and who *say* their children are perfect children, but I really worry about those people! God knows we are not perfect parents; He knew before your children were born that you would not be a perfect parent. That is why the Bible contains help and hope just for you.

If you are a new parent, frightened of making mistakes with that precious child, God brings you hope! If your children are grown, and you are burdened with the knowledge that you were not a perfect parent, it is not too late! In this book, I want to show you the wonderful instruction, encouragement, and, yes, redemption, that God has provided for parents and children! In this book, you will learn that when it comes to being a parent, ***God's way is best!***

Parenting is a huge responsibility. We all need God's help because someone else is also interested in our children: Satan. The devil hates children because they're made in the image of God. Jesus said, " . . . *Except ye . . . become as little children, ye shall not enter into the kingdom of heaven*" (Matthew 18:3). Children are innocent. They are easily swayed, easily led. What does the devil want to do? He wants to destroy children because the children themselves are a symbol of God's kingdom.

In the Old Testament, there are examples of terrible child abuse: they sacrificed children to idols; they caused their children to pass through the fire; if you remember, Pharaoh ordered all the male babies to be thrown into the river. There is even cannibalism in the Old Testament. Women literally ate their children. Children were sold to pay off debts. Remember the story of Elisha and the woman who came to him and said, "I don't know what I'm going to do. I don't have any money, I'm going to have to sell my two boys into slavery in order to pay the debts of my husband." She had a little oil and God multiplied it, working a miracle to save the children.

When the wise men came and said, "We have found the king," Herod ordered the murder of all the male babies under age three! Child abuse is nothing new. The devil hates children, including yours. Keep that in mind, and be aware of what he is trying to do.

On the other hand, *God* wants your children to prosper and become mighty! Isaiah 61:9 says:

And their seed shall be known among the Gentiles and their offspring among the people: all that see them shall acknowledge them, that they are the seed which the LORD hath blessed.

Isn't it wonderful when the world looks at our children and says, "Hey, how did they get that way? What happened that they're doing so well? What happened that they're successful; they're not drug addicts, they're not alcoholics, and they're not living in prostitution?" Then, we can say, "It's the Word of God! It's all because we made a decision that *God's way is best."*

Chapter One
God's Way Is Best

Christians are to be the *mighty* ones! I don't think all the judges should be sinners. I don't think all the governors and mayors should be sinners. I don't think all the congressmen, senators, and presidents should be sinners! *Our children* can have these high positions!

Many people in the Bible held high positions. Look at Daniel. He was a mighty person of faith! He became excellent in three different governments. Somebody trained him well, . . . and guess where that kind of training starts? At home!

Joseph is another good example. Maybe Joseph's father didn't do it all right, but he didn't do it all wrong, either. Joseph really came out well, and became a prime minister to the land of Egypt. Likewise, our children can be mighty, if we make the decision that God's way is best.

Raising Children God's Way

Deciding to follow God's instructions for

child-rearing is a serious commitment. It doesn't mean reading the Word and all those psychology books, and then picking and choosing which parts you want. No! You read the Word, then stay with it.

God promises big breakthroughs for your children. Look at His wonderful promise for your children:

Praise ye the LORD. Blessed is the man that feareth the LORD, that delighteth greatly in his commandments. His seed shall be mighty upon earth: the generation of the upright shall be blessed (Psalms 112:1,2).

Do you want to guarantee your children's success? Then *you* praise the Lord and delight greatly in His commandments. His commandments make your seed mighty upon the earth. When you teach His commandments, you are putting your confidence in God.

I remember one time God dealt with me because I was concerned about my children. They were misbehaving. They wouldn't do this; they wouldn't do that. I tried to teach them, but they didn't seem to be getting it. Haven't we all felt this way sometimes? God said to me, "You be the mother, and I'll be God." Folks, sometimes we need God to say to us, "I'll be God . . . you be the best you can, and I'll do what you can't do." What a comforting promise! When we truly depend on God, He will be right beside us, parenting our children.

You see, God has promised that when we begin to teach the Word, the Word doesn't return void. Later in this book, we're going to explore some principles that will help us teach it better, and in a fashion that children can grasp. We *can* and absolutely *must* create a desire in them to want God and to want to do godly things when they leave us.

When Our Children Desire God

Deuteronomy 6:24 says:

And the LORD commanded us to do all these statutes, to fear the LORD our God, for our good always, that he might preserve us alive, as it is at this day.

His statutes and commandments are for our own good. They are designed to make us good and to improve our lives. If we decide the best way is God's way for our children, we are teaching them for their good, according to God's promise.

God tells us that if we delight in His commandments, if we delight in His statutes, and if we teach them to our children, then our children are going to be mighty and their lives are going to be good. Let's look at some particular things He tells us about our children, and how we are to train them.

The Nature of Children

Children are not born ready-made! Did you know there are two Hebrew words for "child"? One of them is *na'ar*. It means "to growl, to cry, to scream, to roar, to gush, and to agitate." Don't all those describe the natural-born child? This is the description of children from infants to teenagers!

The other Hebrew word for "child" is *ben*. It means "son" or "daughter." *Ben* has a fuller connotation than *na'ar*, which describes only the actions of a child. It describes the *relationship* between a parent and a child.

Now Jesus was never called the *na'ar*, "child," of God. He was called the *ben*, "Son," of God. Why? Because He had a relationship with the Father. When we were made, we were made in the image of God, so a lot of people say we're the children of God. When we are born again, we become the "sons" of God, because we come into a *relationship* with Him. The relationship makes us sons and daughters.

What does God want your children to be? You say, "They growl, they are *na'ar*, they cry, they scream, they roar, they gush, they agitate." Even so, God wants your children to be *ben*, "sons" and "daughters." Because more than taking care of the roars, the screams, the cries, the agitating, He wants you to have a *relationship* with your children.

Children Are Foolish

Proverbs 22:15 says: *"Foolishness is bound in the heart of a child; but the rod of correction shall drive it far from him."*

All children are foolish. They are born that way. They don't know everything. They may have a high IQ, but they don't always make high-IQ decisions. Correct? They kick the side of the crib, throw the bottle out, scream and have temper tantrums. They hit their little brother and sister, lie, steal, and cheat, and you say, "Where'd that come from?" Well, that's foolishness and it's bound in the heart of that child, so you are going to have to deal with it. No matter how sweet they are or how much they look like you, that child is full of foolishness.

Foolishness in Hebrew means "thickness of fluid." Let's just face it: our children are a little thick in the head! So what do we do? It says in Proverbs 22:15 that you are supposed to discipline them. Now, discipline does not eradicate the sinful, foolish nature. The purpose of discipline is to educate. Your major responsibility as a parent is to *educate* that child. Later in this chapter, we'll see the ways that we are to educate them—the ways that Proverbs teaches us.

Telling Behavior

The second thing about a child is that his behavior shows what he is. Look at Proverbs 20:11: *"Even a child is known by his doings, whether his work be pure, and whether it be right."*

Sometimes when your child is tiny, she has quite a temper. You think, "That's from her father. She didn't get that from me, 'cause I'm too sweet for that." Nevertheless, the child's behavior—that temper tantrum, that lying, that pouting—shows her nature.

So what do you have to do? Two things:

(1) When there is good behavior, you have to encourage it.

(2) When there's bad behavior, you have to deal with it.

You deal with it by educating, by training, and by discipline. God gives us several ways that we can deal with the behavior of a child to help them get educated, and to help them get a new nature.

Now, you can't say, "Well, they'll get saved and then everything will be all right." No, they need training *before* they get saved, and they need training *after* they get saved. You know that even you are still in training! We're all under construction, all the time. It never stops.

When children are born, they do not respond to wisdom. They need to be trained to respond to godly wisdom because they weren't born with that ability. I don't like to hear people say, "Just let children express themselves. If they want to pull down the drape, let them pull down the drape. If they want to throw spaghetti all over you, just smile and go take a bath." That is just not true, and it is not right. It is not God's way!

God shows us very clearly that children are not born with a great ability for wisdom. We, as parents, are responsible for putting the wisdom in them. What we put in is what we are going to get out.

Children Are Rebellious

Some place, somewhere along the way, all children are rebellious. There is a well-known evangelist who had two sons and a daughter. His daughter and one son have ministries and so do their mates, but the other son chose not to serve God. That son always resented the fact that his father did a lot of overseas evangelism and travel, so he was always uptight with his father. He got into drugs, and two years ago he died from an overdose. Now, I know this family very well, so I said to the brother who is in evangelism and is doing so well, "Tell me about your brother. Why do you think that he never really wanted to serve God? Why do you think he took the route of rebellion and the route of drugs? You didn't take it, your sister didn't take it. Was it the way your parents handled him? Was it different?"

He said, "No, we were all treated the same way. It was *his* choice."

When it comes down to it, we can say, "This is the way I'm going to train you, I'm going to put all this into you," but eventually it becomes *their* choice. So it's very important that, as much as we can, we educate them early so that they make right choices. When the rubber meets the road though, they have got to make their own choices. We are preparing them to make right choices.

We do that through discipline and training, God's way.

God's Discipline

The book of Proverbs describes three kinds of training or discipline.

1. With the rod

I believe in spanking. I don't believe in abuse, but I believe in spanking.

Proverbs 13:24 says, *"He that spareth his rod hateth his son: but he that loveth him chasteneth him betimes."*

The rod is a part of God's method of child training. Why? Because the child has rebellion, the child has behavior patterns that are not wise, and the child has foolishness. The rod helps to drive foolishness far from him. Even so, the rod is not the major way you train your child.

2. Talking to them

The major way you train your child is verbally. Look at Proverbs 13:1;15:5:

A wise son heareth his father's instruction: but a scorner heareth not rebuke. . . . A fool despiseth his father's instruction: but he that regardeth reproof is prudent.

So a child needs to *hear* instruction. They're not going to hear it from TV or movies like *Lion King* or *Star Wars*. They are going to have to hear it from us. Get them into Sunday School and youth groups, all the things that you can, but *never* think that activities will take the place of what you teach at home. Children have to be taught the Word at home. We teach and teach and teach, by word and by example.

3. Circumstances

In Proverbs 30:17, we are told:

The eye that mocketh at his father, and despiseth to obey his mother, the ravens of the valley shall pick it out, and the young eagles shall eat it.

If children won't listen to instruction, if they won't listen to the rod, God will send circumstances, too, because this is a moral universe.

I remember, Sarah was real mouthy when she was little. We would say to her, "Watch your mouth! It's going to get you into trouble." Every now and then she'd just pop up with something so stupid! One day when she was in third grade, the principal called me from school. I was rather shocked, because her grades were good and she liked school. The principal said, "We had a little problem with Sarah today. She said the teacher was drunk. She told the other students and one of the students told the teacher that Sarah Hickey was telling everybody she was drunk. The teacher brought Sarah into my office because that's a very serious accusation. If that goes home to the parents, this teacher could lose her job. I've talked to Sarah and she's very sorry."

When Sarah got off the bus, she came in the house and just fell into my arms crying. "Mother, my big mouth, my big mouth!" Then she told me what had happened. This teacher would put her head in her hands when she got frustrated. She'd just put her head down. Apparently one of the students said to Sarah, "You know what, she's drunk!" Sarah thought that was really something to tell everybody, so she made it her business to tell the rest of the class. Sarah learned, though. She said, "Mother, I've got a big mouth, but I'm going to keep it under control from now on." Now what helped with that lesson? Circumstances.

God will train and He will use discipline, but if we won't learn, He'll send a circumstance that will get us into shape. As parents, we can train and discipline our children, knowing God will send circumstances to teach our children, too.

You know, that *na'ar*—that child that roars and screams and agitates us—that child is also our son or our daughter. We want to have a relationship that helps them with the roaring, screaming, crying, and agitating. We want something to develop in them that eliminates the *na'ar*, and builds up the *ben*. In Chapter 5, we will explore the importance of this relationship, and how to build it.

Isn't it wonderful that God has given us the gift of children just as He has also given us the ways and methods to raise our children? You know, I always say a loud

"Amen!" when I read III John 4: *"I have no greater joy than to hear that my children walk in truth."* If we can feel this way about our children, then do you realize how God feels about us when He sees us walking in truth? That just rejoices Him!

Chapter Two
The 4-A Method of Training

My son, keep thy father's commandment, and forsake not the law of thy mother: Bind them continually upon thine heart, and tie them about thy neck. When thou goest, it shall lead thee; when thou sleepest, it shall keep thee; and when thou awakest, it shall talk with thee. For the commandment is the lamp; and the law is light; . . . (Proverbs 6:20-23).

These instructions from Solomon to the children of Israel are so important. Notice the different roles of the father and the mother. The father has the lamp (the commandment) and the mother puts the light inside the lamp (the law). The instruction of both parents, based on God's commandments and laws, points the way to a good life. It says here that instruction will be an ornament of grace to your head and chains around your neck. When mother and father get involved, God's Word hits the kids' heads, then it puts the chains around their neck, too, to lead them where they should go.

Most importantly, the Word hits their hearts. That is so important. We don't want our children to follow rules just because we tell them to; we want the Word to be internalized in them. We want them to *want* to do the right thing. The thing we want most of all is for them to have the ability to make right decisions on their own, because the Word is imbedded in their heads and hearts. We don't want them just following the rules, but we want them to LOVE the rules because they know those rules are the way of the Lord, the way of life. That's the desire of every Christian parent.

A Parent's Most Important Gift

Parents like to give their children gifts. Look at Matthew 7:9-11:

Or what man is there of you, whom if his son ask bread, will he give him a stone? Or if he ask a fish, will he give him a serpent? If ye then, being evil, know how to give good gifts unto your children, how much more shall your Father which is in heaven give good things to them that ask him?

God loves to give good gifts to His children, and you do, too. Well, what's the best gift you could give to your child? The very best gift any parent can give a child is the gift of the wisdom of God. There is no better gift than that! You can give them a nice bicycle, but bicycles without wisdom can be deadly. The bicycle can wear out. They outgrow their bicycles and want newer and bigger ones, but the wisdom of God can never wear out. It stays with them forever. Our biggest responsibility, and the most joyous task we can undertake, is to educate our children in Christian principles. When we put the Word in them, we give them a gift that is lasting, something eternal.

The 4-A Treatment (AAAA)

How do we give our children the Word so that it sticks? There are four basic things that children need, and if we deliver their training with these in mind, children will be much more receptive. These four things are:

Authority
Affection
Approval
Acceptance

What does authority of parents over children look like? We've all heard the old saying "spare the rod and spoil the child," but let's look more carefully at the scripture behind that saying: *"He that spareth his rod, hateth his son: but he that loveth him chasteneth him betimes"* (Proverbs 13:24).

Are we supposed to train our children with

rods? Are we supposed to spank children? Yes! But, *how* are we supposed to spank them? I have sometimes spanked them when it didn't come out as well as I expected. You have, too! So I began to look at this scripture more closely. What is it about authority that is so important? You have to get hold of the desire of your heart. Do you want immediate behavior change or do you want a long-term heart change?

You can spank them, and they can say, "OK, I won't do it for now," but when you turn your back, ten days later they do the same thing again. They think, "As long as Mom doesn't know, if I can get away from Dad, I'm gonna do it." What we really want is a heart change, so that they won't *want* to do that wrong thing again. We want to train them to have an *appetite* for what is good. When we discipline, then, we're going to have to discipline them very carefully. If you discipline in wrong ways, you are going to get wrong results. You could use the rod and not get the long-term heart change, and, in fact, that's what happens many, many times.

Here are two more scriptures to help us understand the use of spankings in disciplining our children: *"Foolishness is bound in the heart of a child; but the rod of correction shall drive* it far from him" (Proverbs 22:15) and *"The rod and reproof give wisdom: but a child left to himself bringeth his mother to shame"* (Proverbs 29:15).

When we discipline, we are driving out the natural foolishness of the child. But much more importantly, we are replacing that foolishness with wisdom. We have to be very, very careful in discipline, so that it results in wisdom. Discipline must be done carefully, and it must be done with love.

Affection with Authority

Children need love, and they need that love to be expressed affectionately. Everybody, even a doctor, will tell you that you should breast feed children. Isn't that kind of the fad now? You know, I think breast feeding immediately exposes a child to love and affection because there is intimacy with the mother. Mother breast feeds the baby, she cuddles the baby, and all these things have a lot to do with touching.

I believe we need to snuggle our children. We need to love on our children. I think children need love until we die. I'm talking about petting them, patting them, hugging them, squeezing them, saying, "I love you." Why? Because if we show them affection, then our authority is stronger! Affection with authority is the key. We have to have the combination of both, or it's not going to work. So when we are loving them, hugging them, then we can speak into their lives because our love makes them open to our authority. Discipline without affection will not change the heart, and affection without discipline will not teach wisdom. That's why God's authority in our lives works so well with those who are really secure in His love. Christians who deeply believe that God loves them, and who have learned to trust in that love, are open to learning His wisdom. We are even *eager* to learn His Word, because it makes us happy. It makes us happy because we know that God loves us. Isn't it wonderful the way this works?

There are two other things that children need.

Approval and Acceptance

Along with affection and authority, all children want to be accepted. We all like to be accepted by our peers. We like to be accepted in our work positions, but you know, the people from whom we want acceptance and approval the most are our parents. I think all of us are like that. We all remember how wonderful it was when we were growing up and our parents told us they were proud of us. We really blossomed under that approval.

If we give enough acceptance, and we give it consistently, our children will not have to look for so much approval from their peers. They won't get into a lot of worldly things because they're getting so much approval at home. We don't lie to them. We have to tell the truth. When they keep their room neat say, "You are really doing a good job on your room. I'm proud of you." Look for the opportunity to say, "Look at your grades! Why, you have brought this grade up one whole point. Last term you had a "C" and now you've brought it up to a 'B.' Aren't you smart! You are really good!"

My mother used to say this crazy thing to me when I was growing up. I would say to her, "Oh, I just can't make it. I really want to get an A in this subject, but I just can't make it."

She would always reply, "Oh, you can do it."

"Well, how do you know I can do it?" I'd ask her.

She would always say, "You were a smart baby."

I heard that all my life. I always believed that I was a smart baby and smart babies grow up to be smart adults. I grew up on "You were a smart baby." Now, I don't know if I was *really* a smart baby. Probably I was a very normal, ordinary baby, but my mother thought I was smart—at least that's what she told me. That was acceptance and approval. I am sure that a lot of what I have accomplished in my life happened because my mother filled me with this sense that I was capable.

Even when we are older, we look for acceptance from our parents. We really appreciate that acceptance and approval even after the death of our parents. We can put that kind of input into our children with, "I accept you. I accept you for your talents, your abilities. I accept you even when you blow it. I accept you. I love you. I approve of you!" When we show approval of the good things that they do, our discipline will get the mileage that it needs. Without it, we don't get that kind of mileage.

Every parent needs to remember: **A**ffection with **A**uthority brings **A**pproval and **A**cceptance. If we show affection when we are giving authority, it will help a child to receive it, because he feels accepted and approved.

Do you remember when God bragged on Job in front of the devil? God said to the devil, "Devil, have you noticed my servant Job? He flees evil. He loves righteousness. He pursues godly things." Now that's a nice compliment, isn't it? Don't we all long for that kind of approval from our heavenly Father? Many times God would like to say to you "I'm proud of you. You could have lied in that situation and you didn't do it." We all want to hear Him to say, "Well, done, thou good and faithful servant. Enter into your rest."

God likes to say good things about His children. God sent an angel one time to Daniel and he told Daniel three times, "Did you know you're the beloved of the Lord?" How do you think that made Daniel feel? How would you like it if you heard, "God just wants you to know that He is really wild over you!"? How many of you think you'd like that?

I think God would like to tell all of us that He's wild over us. I think He is pleased with a whole lot of things that we do. Maybe we didn't do everything right with our children. I know that I didn't. God told me one time, "You didn't do it all wrong, either. You did a lot of things right, and you are going to get some of the promises with some of the right things. You've repented of the wrong things you did, so don't repent again." (I had repented at least a thousand times!)

There is something powerful about that parental approval. Some of Esau's words hurt me when I read them in the Bible. You can feel his heart reaching out when Jacob got the blessing from their father that he thought was his. He comes to his father and says, "Don't you have a blessing left for me?"

Isaac prophesies over him, but it is not the blessing that Jacob got. Then, for the rest of Esau's life, you see him doing some things that really grieve his parents. He married a Hittite woman and then he married another daughter of Ishmael. He saw that his parents didn't like it so he said, "Oh well, I better get another wife—somebody they'll like."

He constantly wanted their approval, and he didn't get their approval. He didn't get the blessing for which he yearned.

Whenever we can plant acceptance and approval in our children it does something so powerful that lasts all their lives.

Chapter Three
The 5-P's of Successful Parenting

Children need affection, they need you to take authority, and they need acceptance and approval. Parenting is an enormous responsibility, and it takes both parents to do it. Some children respond easily, others don't. For some children, it takes hard knocks before they get it. Some children seem like they never will get it until, through circumstances and the supernatural, God penetrates. Parents have needs, too, though, and God meets those needs wonderfully. Now we are going to look at how God meets the needs of parents, which I like to call the "Five P's":

Principles
Prayer
Peace
Praise
Possibilities

It's unfortunate, but it has become clear to me that we as parents are going to have to become streetwise in these days we live in. When we begin to teach our children the Word of God, it keeps them away from wrong things. There are so many tragic, sad things in this world just lying in wait for our children, and God's principles will help keep them safe.

Let's look at the principles God gives us to teach our children in Proverbs 4:11, *"I have taught thee in the way of wisdom; I have led thee in the right paths."*

Right paths in Hebrew means "the furrows made by a wagon." We parents are that wagon. We make the trails for our children to follow. In other words, if you're going to teach your children right paths, you're going to have to walk in right paths yourself. You can't say, "Don't smoke," to your children while you're lighting up a cigarette yourself. If you tell your child, "I want you to read your Bible," then she is going to say to you, "Are you reading yours, Mom?" A parent who admonishes a child that "I want you to be a person of prayer," must be ready for the child's question: "Why aren't you a person of prayer, Dad?" Children follow examples, and they especially follow the examples of their parents. You cannot get away with "Do as I say, not as I do!" In fact, your actions will make a much deeper impression on your children than anything you can possibly say to them.

Get your kids involved in everything spiritual that you can, but *you* must also get involved! These are formative years. What you put in is what you are going to get out. You make those wagon tracks so that your children have something to follow when they are grown.

Some of you are thinking: "Well, I put in a lot and I'm not getting out very much." I want to encourage you. Don't give up! There's hope! One time Sarah got interested in a guy who wasn't saved. She said, "Well, he's just a friend." However, I kept thinking something was just not right. Of course, when they are 23 and 24 years old, children are not asking for your advice; they don't even want your advice! So I prayed about it. I said, "God, I don't feel good about this." The Lord gave me a scripture from James, "Don't make friends with the world." The Lord said to me, "Tell her this scripture."

I thought, "Oh God, no, no! I will not be popular. We have a good relationship. No, I don't want to. *You* tell her the scripture!"

The Lord replied, "No, I gave it to you. You tell her."

So the next day, I said to Sarah, "God gave me a scripture for you."

She said, "Oh, wonderful!"

33

You can just imagine how enthusiastic she was to hear this! I almost backed out, but I remembered the instructions God gave me, and I went ahead, even though I knew she would be angry at me. After I told her, she said, "I don't appreciate that."

Believe me, I knew from the way she looked at me, and the way she stomped out of the house, that it definitely wasn't appreciated. For about three days I got the "cool" treatment. Then, Sarah came to me and said, "Mother, God really dealt with me about what you said. I asked Him, 'Lord, why didn't You give *me* the scripture? Why'd You have to tell my mother? I'm here. Why didn't You tell me?' He said, 'Because you needed someone to be accountable to you or you wouldn't listen.' "

God has given us the *principles* of His wisdom; and if we plant it early, it will pay off when our children get older. Prayer turns us toward Him when we just don't have any answers ourselves.

Praying Parents in the Bible

Prayer changes your children, but prayer is so powerful and so wonderful that it also changes you most of all. Someone showed me a book that gave the average amount of time that pastors spent in prayer in different nations. It said in New Zealand, the average amount of prayer a day was 22 minutes. The United States was about 14 minutes. Isn't that sad? In Korea, the average prayer time for pastors was about an hour a day. I can assure you that Wally and I, and every pastor in Wally's church, prays at least an hour a day, and maybe more. Prayer is very important if we want to see our children come through.

Look at Hannah. She prayed, and she received Samuel as a result. Plus, she received five more children. Her firstborn, Samuel, became a tremendous man of prayer, one of the greatest intercessors in the Bible. God listed Samuel with Moses and Job, the highest men of God.

Where did Samuel get into this prayer? We know he loved God as a child. We know he was very soft, very tender to the voice of God. I think that Samuel's heart for prayer started with Hannah. She left Samuel with Eli, but it wasn't a very good environment, surrounded by Eli's bratty sons. Remember, Eli was overindulgent and very partial to his children, but Samuel stayed true and sensitive to God. How did that happen?

Hannah just kept praying. You see, prayer will put a guard around your children. Prayer will take care of your children when you can't be with them. Folks, once they're five and six years old, they walk out that door and they're not with you. Your prayers can bring protection and watch over them to keep them.

And I believe that when Hannah made the little coats that she sent to Samuel every year, they were almost like prayer cloths. I think Hannah had prayed over every stitch as she wove and sewed, and when Samuel put that coat on, I think it was like an anointed prayer cloth all over him. He must have felt the prayers of his mother, and her prayers carried him in that terrible environment at Eli's house. When we pray, our children will pray. That kind of prayer stays with our children. If you want them to pray, then YOU must pray. Your prayer will be caught by them.

Job prayed for his children. David prayed for his children. Prayer will fill in the cracks where we cannot fill in the cracks, but there's something else that parents can bring that is very powerful to their children.

God Promises You Rest

Except the LORD build the house, they labour in vain that build it: except the LORD keep the city, the watchman waketh but in vain. It is vain for you to rise up early, to sit up late, to eat the bread of sorrows: for so he giveth his beloved sleep (Psalms 127:1,2).

I've always taken that second verse and thought, "Wow! I should be resting at night. This is a good scripture for sleepless parents." This is for parents who are worried when their teenagers are out late. How many of you have had your child walk out and then worried until they came back in? It wasn't that they were late, or anything was wrong, or God was calling you. You were just nervous and worried. I know mothers are especially like this. I would never go to sleep until Sarah was in. I would hear the dog bark, the key in the door, and then I'd go to sleep. Wally, though, would go right to sleep! He was bever bothered. Why is that? Usually mothers lie awake at night, until the children are all safely home.

This verse says that you shouldn't be worrying so much. You need to trust God. There comes a time and a place where you've got to trust God. God's going to build your house. God's going to keep the city. If you to chew your nails and fall apart and have a nervous breakdown, that is not trusting God. Trust God with your children and He will give you *peace*. Is there anything parents need more than the peace of the Lord?

When I am worrying about my children, I like to turn to Psalms 42:5:

Why art thou cast down, O my soul? and why art thou disquieted in me? hope thou in God: for I shall yet praise him for the help of his countenance.

The only One we can look to for help with our worries about our children is God. We can teach the Word, we can pray. We're going to make mistakes. We may not do as much praying as we should. We may not be producing enough godly wisdom in them— or, we may be doing all these things in great quantity. It still has to come down to one thing: your hope must be in God. We can always praise Him because just the simple act of praising His name fills us with His peace and His wisdom.

God has given us wise principles to teach our children, and He has given us prayer, peace, and praise. Isn't God wonderful? He knows exactly what we worried, harried, hassled parents need!

God Provides for the Future

When you begin praying and praising, something opens up inside you, especially in Spirit-filled believers, that raises you into a new realm. This is a prophetic realm: seeing ahead for your children. Now, I'm not talking about *your* ambitions for your children; I'm talking about what the *Spirit* wants to put on your children.

The Bible gives us some examples of fathers who prophesied the future over their sons. Isaac prophesied over his son, Jacob, when he gave Jacob the blessing. How did Isaac do that? Because he was a man of prayer with a close relationship with God, he could see what the Spirit had for his son's future.

Later, when Jacob was dying, he prophesied over all 12 of his own sons. Those prophesies came to pass down the line. For example, Jacob said, *"The scepter shall not depart from Judah . . . "* (Genesis 49:10). Sure enough, Judah would produce the major kings of Israel. Jesus Christ, the King of kings would come from the tribe of Judah.

Jacob said: *"Benjamin shall ravin as a wolf: in the morning he shall devour the prey, and at night he shall divide the spoil"* (Genesis 49:27).

Benjamin produced Saul, the first king. Benjaminites often got "off track" in God's plan; but the Apostle Paul, who wrote 13 epistles, was of the tribe of Benjamin. He divided the spoil. His ancestor Jacob prophesied that very thing that came to pass, because Jacob entered into the Spirit.

There is something in each of us that wants the blessing of our father, our natural father. Something in us also wants the blessing of the heavenly Father. Children love to be complimented by their father, and want his blessing. That longing, I believe, is the spiritual call for the blessing for the future. In the heart of every parent is a place where God can drop in His prophesy for their child or children and their future. He can cause them to speak the words of blessing and the anointed Word of God that can cause that child to enter into the inheritance that God has for them in the future.

There are tremendous possibilities for our children on this earth! If we only look at the impossibilities, we are going to be depressed every day, but the Word says that the seed of the righteous shall be delivered. All the promises are there for your children, and your children's children, and all that the Lord shall call from far off. All these promises are delivered in the baptism of the Holy Spirit. You may say, "Well, my children are just not into the baptism of the Spirit." Some of you are grieving because your children have said that they will never be Christians. Ignore them. Who are you going to believe—your children or the Word of God? Wave your worries goodbye. Just say, "God, they are going to become Christians. Devil leave them alone." Then, begin to enter into possibility thinking, because if you claim the possibilities with the principles of the Word, with prayer, praising God constantly, and claiming the peace that He has promised you, then God's provisions will be fulfilled.

Reject the Guilt

These days, it seems that the world is always burdening parents with guilt. Do you ever feel that way? If you start feeling guilty because you are not a perfect parent, remember that guilt is not from God! When guilt is overwhelming you, it's time to turn to His Word. The Bible is full of valuable instruction—and it is full of comfort and encouragement, too.

We are going to look at some parents in the Bible who weren't perfect parents but who still had some good results. I want to encourage you, because I think parents have enough guilt and worry piled on them. All we have to do is look at our kids to feel the heavy burden. That's why it is so important for parents to turn to the Word. We need the encouragement of the Word, we need the anointing of God, and most of all, we need the wisdom of God.

41

Together, we are going to examine Biblical parents, and how they coped with the same problems we have today: foolish, rebellious children whose behavior is less than perfect.

Parents Who Play Favorites

When you have several children and some of them really behave and one of them really misbehaves, it's hard not to be partial. Look at Isaac. There is no question he was partial to Esau. He liked Esau. Esau liked sports and the outdoors and Esau would kill the wild meat that Isaac liked to eat. He was attracted to Esau, his son. They seemed to have a very good relationship. He was much more partial toward him than toward Jacob. Yet Jacob and Esau were twins!

On the other hand, we have the mama, Rebecca, who was partial toward Jacob. This was not a good thing, but the results turned out good for Jacob. Partiality didn't ruin him because God got hold of his life. You may make mistakes with your children—we all do—but if we can trust God, God can bring our children through. God will do what you can't do, what you didn't do, or what you failed at doing.

I'm not trying to give you excuses to get off the hook; I just want you to know that God can move where you cannot move. What was the difference between Jacob and Esau? Jacob loved God, and Jacob was willing to make a commitment to God, and willing to let God deal with him. Esau never did have much respect for God. Anyone who would sell their birthright for a bowl of stew is absolutely stupid. Maybe Isaac and Rebecca didn't handle parenthood well, but they had some good results. Is it possible you are partial toward one of your children? You need to let God give you wisdom and not continue in some of these things. At the same time, if you made some mistakes, that doesn't mean it's the end.

Now, Jacob had some partiality, too. He was very partial toward Joseph and Benjamin. The other 10 boys were the pits. They were big-time problems. Reuben was sleeping around with wrong women. Oh, the trouble Jacob had with those kids! Yet we see that they began to develop and God began to pull them out and make something out of them. God can take kids who are rebels and parents who have blown it, and God can still bring something good out of the situation because God deals in the miraculous!

Spoiling Children

Some of us are too indulgent with our children: too much affection and not enough authority. In the Bible, there was a parent who was very indulgent with his children—and who was warned about it. Eli was very indulgent with his children. It was sad, because basically Eli loved God and he was a good priest. Although he was a spiritual man, when it came to his children, Eli didn't draw any lines or any limitations. Finally, in I Samuel 2:29, an unnamed prophet came to him and said, "If you don't shape up with your children, you're going to lose the priesthood for your household."

Unfortunately, Eli ignored this terrible warning.

Next, Samuel came and heard the audible voice of God and said the same thing to him (I Samuel 3:13-18). Again, Eli failed to heed the warning. He was more partial to his children than he was to God, and as a result, he lost his children. One of his grandsons was even named *Ichabod*, which means "the glory of God has departed." Being a parent is very serious. Partiality and being very indulgent are very serious, but you don't have to stay like that. When you know the truth, the truth can set you free.

When we have warnings and we see weaknesses, and the Holy Spirit shows us what we need to do, it's time to listen. We just can't say, "Well, somehow it will all come out right anyway." That's not a good attitude. We need to change what the Holy Spirit shows us to change. Remember, God can do what you cannot do.

God's Number One Priority for Parents

What is the number-one thing God wants us to do as parents? I would say He wants us to be educators. In Proverbs, Solomon talks about how his parents educated him:

My son, hear the instruction of thy father, and forsake not the law of thy mother: For they shall be an ornament of grace unto thy head, and chains about thy neck (Proverbs 1:8,9).

Our number-one priority, then, must be to provide a Christian education and lifestyle for our children. Now, I'm not talking about Christian schools. Christian schools can be wonderful, but they cannot put Christianity in your children because, frankly, they just have them for a certain amount of time. You've got them in the morning, at night, on weekends, and vacations. Most importantly, Christianity has to come into our children out of our relationship with them. Most of the Christian teaching, most of the Christian principles, most of the Christian living, has to start in the home, and it has to start with us.

It is best for both parents to be involved in the Christian education of your children. Men are very different about what they train a child to do compared with what a mother's going to train the child to do. The roles of the two parents are different, yet both are guiding and nurturing the children to grow up so that when they leave home, they follow the right path.

Fathers and Mothers Are Different

In the beginning of Genesis, when God made Adam, He assigned him a task. He created men to be producers, problem solvers, and achievers. God said, "Adam, I want you to take dominion. I want you to take care of this great big garden. I want you to name all the animals." Then God saw that Adam was lonely, so God took Eve out of Adam.

Now, when He made Eve, it wasn't to take care of the garden all the time. Eve wasn't made to name the animals. Eve was made to have a relationship with Adam. Women love relationships. They always want to talk, talk, talk to men. They want communication. Men think, "I said it, that's enough. That settles it." A woman will come to a husband and say, "Oh, this terrible thing is going on in our neighborhood. This woman is doing this, she's doing that. Her husband is doing this and doing that." Her husband says, "Well, they should do these three things. One, two, three." Now, she doesn't want a solution—she wants to talk—and her husband doesn't understand that.

Traveling with your husband, you can see a sign for a restaurant and say, "Aren't you thirsty?"

The husband says, "Nope" and just drives on.

Well, that's not really what you had in mind. You want him to say, "Do you want something to drink?" Finally you say, "I've wanted something to drink for the last twenty miles" and he is amazed! He says, "Well, why didn't you say so?"

All this is because we are made differently. Isn't that true? Women love relationships and men love achievements and solutions. Yet we are supposed to get together to raise a child! You see, though, those very traits in a husband can be so strong and so powerful. They are essential for teaching a child how to achieve, how to solve problems. The father can teach children to draw the lines and keep walking the right way, how to see things clearly—calling things by their right names! The mother's primary role is in nurturing and teaching children how to build and maintain relationships.

God gave children both mothers and fathers because children need the training and love of both. God gave those mothers and fathers everything they need to bring their children through, in spite of our mistakes. He gave us:

Principles

Prayer

Peace

Praise

and

Possibilities

As parents, it is our responsibility to give our children what they need:

Authority

Affection

Approval

and

Acceptance

Parents, God wants to soak you with His love, so His love can overflow into your children. If you don't come under God's authority, what makes you think your children are going to come under yours? I want my children and your children to serve God! Remember, it all starts at home, with us not only saying it but doing it.

Let's start right now, with prayer, and praise, and possibility thinking. Say this prayer now, and every day you spend as a parent.

Father, help me to be the parent You want me to be. I know Your ways are best. Help me to be sensitive to Your voice, to Your wisdom. Lord, I'm not just driving foolishness out of my children; I am replacing it with Your wisdom. Lord, I give You my children. I believe they are going to be mighty seed on this earth, just as you have promised. Thank You, today, for breakthroughs in my children and breakthroughs in me. Help me to remember, every day, that Your ways are best. My children will obey You quickly, and quietly, because I'll train them and they'll see me walk the same way. Thank You, Lord, for helping me. You are God, I am the parent. I'll do my best and You'll do the supernatural. In Jesus' name. Amen.

Chapter Four
Five Principles of Skillful Discipline

Have you ever thought of your children as arrows? Look at the way that Psalms 127:4,5 talks about our children:

As arrows are in the hand of a mighty man; so are children of the youth. Happy is the man that hath his quiver full of them: they shall not be ashamed, but they shall speak with the enemies in the gate.

The more I thought about this strange description, the more I liked it. You know, children really are like arrows. We try to make them strong, pointing them in the right direction, and then we pray that they will hit the target!

If you are making an arrow, you know you have to find a straight stick. All sticks have some little lumps and bumps in them, so you have to peel certain pieces off, smooth them down and straighten them out, if they are going to hit their targets.

51

Every parent has a desire for their children to hit those targets that God has planned for them. We must, however, realize that God's promises are not fulfilled unless His conditions are met. What are some of these conditions? One of the first conditions is that children obey their parents.

Children, obey your parents in the Lord: for this is right. Honour thy father and mother; (which is the first commandment with promise;)That it may be well with thee, and thou mayest live long on the earth (Ephesians 6:1-3).

The Benefits of Discipline

Our children must learn to obey, and it is our job to teach them. The method that God gives us to teach them is discipline. Discipline is not punishment; it is instruction.

The Bible says:

He that spareth his rod hateth his son. . . The rod and reproof give wisdom: but a child left to himself bringeth his mother to shame.

When we discipline, we are preparing children to be wise. The result of that wisdom is the security we all experience when we are given clear boundaries. Proverbs 15:5 tells us, *"A fool despiseth his father's instruction: but he that regardeth reproof is prudent."* Instruction means setting boundaries.

I like boundaries. If I am a guest speaker at a new church, I always ask them how long they want me to speak and what they want me to do. Sometimes the pastor says, "I don't care, do whatever you want to do." That always makes me nervous. I have to have some boundaries because sometimes I go ahead and do everything I want to do and afterwards the pastor says, "I wish you hadn't done that. We never have an altar call." I would much rather have known those boundaries up front. Boundaries give me the security and the confidence of knowing what is expected of me.

As parents, we must set boundaries for our children. People say that loving your children is enough, but that isn't enough if, like many, your idea of love is just permissiveness. Some so-called experts say that we should "Let the little darlings express themselves. Let them pull the drapes down and spill spaghetti all over you." That is not God's way, though!

God's Way Includes Discipline

God says only fools ignore boundaries: *"He that begetteth a fool doeth it to his sorrow: and the father of a fool hath no joy"* (Proverbs 17:21).

Children who are "expressing" themselves are expressing their sin natures. We must try to get that sin nature out, and the new nature in, and that takes instruction, time, and discipline. Sometimes it is painful, but it is more painful to have a child that acts like a fool.

When we teach the fear of God with the wisdom of God, it gives our children a refuge. When the prodigal got into trouble, what did he do? He ran back home, because he knew that home provided refuge. He knew the limitations that his father set in that home, and in those limitations, he found a safe refuge.

As a parent, you will also have a peaceful and secure refuge when your children know their limitations. When they grow up and leave home, if you know that your children have learned the limitations, it gives you peace— the peace of knowing that your children are walking with God.

The Bible teaches that we should discipline our children. We are to love them in truth, the truth of the Word. Therefore, we must love our children by teaching them the truth and living with them in truth.

What is our role as parents? It is to teach our children God's way, so that they have a long life on the earth, and it goes well with them while they are here. If they don't obey and honor their parents, it is not going to go well for them, and they're not going to live a long and good life. For these reasons, it is very important that we apply ourselves to teaching our children obedience.

Teaching Our Children Obedience

Have you ever seen a child who was just born and then spontaneously obeyed? No, of course not! Children are born with foolishness. They are born with a carnal nature. We must teach them to obey. How do we teach them to obey? We teach them to obey *quickly* and *quietly*.

If we teach our children to obey the first time we speak, they will probably obey God the first time He speaks. If we have to scream to get their attention, then that's probably what God is going to have to do, too. We must teach them that we mean what we say. We must correct them immediately when they misbehave, and we must do it softly, calmly, quietly.

We shouldn't do it with bribery. We don't say, "If you behave when I take you out, I'll give you a candy bar." That is not the key to getting children to obey. Instead, we teach them that when they obey, it makes people like them and it will give them success and acceptance.

Samuel Learned Obedience

Samuel's mother must have taught him to obey quickly and quietly, because when he began hearing that voice, he jumped right up. He didn't say, "I don't want to come, I'm sleeping." He jumped right up and went to Eli. Eli said to him, "I didn't call you." Samuel went back to bed. Then again the voice said, "Samuel, Samuel," and he jumped up again. He didn't say, "I'm tired of hearing voices calling my name. I've worked hard all day." He jumped up again and ran to Eli. This time Eli said, "Maybe it's God speaking to you."

Eli didn't raise his voice and say, "Samuel, I told you a hundred times that when God calls your name, you are supposed to say, 'Here am I.'" Eli just quietly said, "Say, 'Here am I.'" Samuel went back, and God again said, "Samuel, Samuel." This time, Samuel said, "I am your servant, Lord. Just talk to me." God called Samuel quietly, and Samuel obeyed quickly! All through Samuel's life, you see him obeying quickly and quietly. His mother had taught him how to hear God's still, small voice.

I have noticed that most of the time, God doesn't yell at me. He doesn't say, "MARILYN!" When he wants to get my attention, He speaks very softly. It's easy to miss that quiet voice, so let's not yell at our children. Let's teach them quickly and quietly. Let's help them learn to listen to God that way, too, so that God won't have to yell to get their attention.

Five Rules for Successful Discipline

Let's look at five simple methods for skillful discipline:

1) Always be in control of yourself. Don't discipline when you are out of control. If you are very angry when you deal with your children, the only response you are going to get from them is more anger. Discipline is a delicate art, and we can't concentrate on what is best for our children if we have lost our own composure. If you need to, walk away and count to ten—or count to 1,000 if you have to! Tell your child, "We will talk about this later, when I am not so angry with you."

2) Deal quickly when they have done something wrong. Don't let it go. If you have several little ones at home, you may be so tired that the battle just doesn't seem worth it. You *must not* let children get away with breaking your rules, not even once. In order for the discipline to be immediate, it must be done by the parent who sees the misbehavior. It doesn't work when a mother says, "Just wait until your father gets home!" Then when he gets home, she says, "You need to spank Joe and you need to spank Suzy." Now that poor father is tired, and he didn't see how Joe or Suzy misbehaved, so when he spanks the children, he is not doing it out of a heart of love for them; he is just doing it to avoid a fight with his wife! The parent who sees the misbehavior should be the one to apply the discipline.

3) Correct to effect change. The purpose of discipline is not to tear children down and make them feel worthless. The purpose is to correct them, so that their behavior will improve. Be sure that you tell them that it is the *behavior* that is bad. You *love* them, but you dislike that bad behavior. Talk about "bad behavior," not "bad children."

No behavior will improve if you let kids get away with bad behavior sometimes. Kids are amazing! They will try everything to get away with bad behavior. They will play one parent against the other. They will ask you to do something when you have company because they think that in front of company you will say "Yes." You must work hard to be consistent. A behavior that was wrong yesterday is also wrong today and it will still be wrong tomorrow. You have to keep repeating your discipline. This is very, very important.

4) Never take away their self-esteem.
When you are disciplining, your purpose is never to make them feel that they are worthless or "no good." You should say, "I know you can do this better, and so I'm disciplining you so that you can do better things."

Words have more effect on children than blows. Words last longer than blows. Cruel words are as abusive to a child as beatings.

We need to show our children that there are rewards for good behavior. People will want to be around you when you behave properly. No one wants to be around wild kids that kick you in the shins! We don't like bad behavior in teenagers, either. If we don't train our children, we are setting them up to be rejected.

5) Praise in public, discipline in private.
Discipline in public can be crushing to a child. What if a child is acting up in public? You must take them some place away from people. Maybe you can put them in the car. Then, you can say, "We are going to get this straightened out, right here and right now." It's very important that we deal with those things, but not publicly.

It can be very damaging to children to hear you talking about their bad behavior to others. If he hears you telling a friend, "I just want to tell you what Johnny did. Last week, he was beating on his sister, stole her doll, wrecked her tricycle, and I really gave him a good spanking." Now, if Johnny hears you say that, he is going to believe that the person you talked to about him is going to look down on him. Then he will begin to look down on himself. It lowers his self-esteem.

Nobody likes to be called down in public. Do you want to be corrected in public? Treat your children the way you want to be treated.

Your children are very valuable to you and to God. It is essential that you teach them how much you value them. Before you discipline them, you need to say to your children, "I want to tell you, I am disciplining you because I love you so much." Now, they won't believe that at the time, but someday they will realize that you are telling the truth. I have found even in working with adults, that if they know you love them, you can tell them almost anything.

Chapter Five
When Children Rebel

As important as discipline is, it will not work unless you also have a relationship with your child. Putting Christian principles into your child will cost time. It will mean turning off the TV and listening to what they have to say. It will mean going to their games. It will mean paying attention to their interests. You're going to have to take an interest in them if you are going to gain *their* interest in you.

All the discipline, all the rules in the world will not work unless you have a good relationship with your children. In fact, rules without that relationship will bring rebellion. To teach your children, you must use discipline and you must use circumstances, but all of this will be meaningless if you don't have a relationship. If they don't have a relationship with you, then they're going to rebel against you. That relationship can hold them when nothing else can.

Look at the story of the Prodigal Son. He eventually came back to his father. Why did he come back? He knew the rules of his father's house and left home because of those rules. He had taken all of his inheritance and spent it all, so why did he come back? He came back because his father had taken the time during the son's childhood to build a relationship. It was that relationship which pulled him back home.

Try Listening

Children can break a lot of rules and do a lot of stupid things. You, together with circumstances, can discipline them, but will they come back to your love, or will they run away from your rules? Building a relationship with your child means listening to them. That means *really listening*—not stopping them every few seconds to lecture to them. When they start to tell you things, you need to show respect for their thoughts and ideas, and never, ever look shocked!

I remember when one of my children said to me, "Mother, I want you to know that I've been trying beer." I almost fell on the floor and had a fit, but the Lord spoke to me, "Be cool. Don't blow it."

Instead, I asked, "Oh, really? What made you do that?"

"Aren't you shocked?" my child asked.

"Well, yes," I replied, "but I have confidence in you that you will not continue, because you know the consequences of drinking. I have great confidence that this was just a little test, but nothing that you would want to do on a regular basis." We got both children through high school without the alcohol problem. In fact, I heard my child say to a friend on the phone, "My mother has confidence in me. I can't go to the party."

My mother pulled the same thing on me. My mother started saying when I was ten years old, "I know you will never smoke, because you are wise; you make wise decisions, and you know that smoking is not good for you." I was 16 when my best friend started smoking, so I started smoking, too. Then my mother's words came to me, "I know you will never smoke because you are so wise." I never could get into smoking. I thought, "Forget it, I can't stand this stuff." My mother's confidence in me kept me out of smoking, drinking, and lots of other worldly things I could have gotten involved in. Her confidence in me, her *relationship* with me, brought me through.

Solomon says in Proverbs that his mother and father taught him. He said, *"For I was my father's son, tender and only beloved in the sight of my mother"* (Proverbs 4:4). He really had a good relationship with both his mother and his father. They taught him, "Whatever you do, get wisdom." After he became a king, God came to him in the night and asked, "What do you want, Solomon?"

Solomon replied, "Wisdom!" He was programmed for that, and it came out of his relationship with his parents.

Now, Solomon was not a perfect son. He really got off-base sometimes, like when he married so many wrong women. Ecclesiastes shows, however, that he got back on base. That's the power of a good relationship between a child and his parents: it pulls a child back onto the right path, again and again.

The sad part about Solomon is that he did not build that same relationship with his son Rehoboam, who later took the throne after Solomon died. Now, Rehoboam had everything going for him, because he had all of the wisdom that Solomon had written down. He had tremendous wealth; the kingdom of Israel was at its peak. He asked his counselors, "What should I do? Should I keep taxing the people? My father taxed the people very heavily."

His older counselors answered, "No, don't do it. It's not a good thing to do, because you need to have a relationship with the people.

You don't know the people that well, and they don't know you. If you are heavy with rules when you don't have a relationship, they'll rebel against you."

Then Rehoboam called in his younger counselors, and asked what he should do. They answered, "Put it on them. Let them know who's boss. You're the king. Double the tax." Rehoboam didn't listen to the older counselors; he didn't believe that he needed a relationship with the people. He believed all he needed was rules.

Did your father ever say to you, "Because I said so! I'm the father, and you will do what I say"? Did it really make you mad? What if your father had said to you, "The reason I don't want you to do this is because it's not good for you. This is what could happen . . . "? It would have been easier for you to hear and obey him, wouldn't it?

Most of us would have taken it better if our parents had taken the time to treat us with that kind of respect. When parents just say, "I'm the leader here. You do what I say," it always causes rebellion down the line, because they're not building a *relationship;* they are just setting the rules.

So Rehoboam taxed the people. He said, "I want you to know I am the king, and if you think it was hard under my father, you're really going to have it hard under me. I'm going to double the taxation!" And he doubled it.

The result was predictable. Ten tribes split away from him, and went with another man called Jeroboam, so that Rehoboam only had two tribes left. The sad thing is that this never had to happen. It would have been so much better if Rehoboam had gone in there and said, "Look, I'm the king, and I want to do what's best for you because I love you. I know my father taxed you really heavily. We're very prosperous now, so I'm going to lighten up on the taxes. Let's just really commit ourselves to make our nation the best. Let's walk in godly ways." If he had put his energy into his relationship with the people, and his relationship with God, he would have never lost his kingdom.

Many times we lose our children for the same reasons. We've got all the rules: we make them go to church, read their Bibles, clean their rooms. If we scream at them and we never listen to them, if they are afraid to tell us when they make a mistake, then all those rules will do more harm than good. We should have rules—they're important—but we must have the relationship, too. Relationship and rules go together.

When parents say, "You can't smoke, you can't drink, or you can't take drugs, you can't go to this, you can't do that," children are going to rebel in most cases. Making rules is easy. What is not so easy is loving your children, no matter what they say, no matter what they do. Unconditional love is the key to a true relationship.

The perfect model of a relationship is the one we are meant to have with Jesus Christ. People who just go to church and make rules for themselves and for others don't have a relationship with Jesus. They just have religion. Religion is rules without a relationship. Religion says, "Don't do this, don't do that." When you have Jesus in your heart, it's an entirely different thing.

When you have a relationship with Him, you *want* to live a godly life. You do the right thing, not because He's yelling at you, but because you have Jesus in your heart. The stronger your relationship with Jesus, the more you follow the rules. The weaker your relationship with Him, the more you break the rules.

It works the same way with parents and children. The stronger relationship we have with our children, the more they're going to keep the rules. You build that relationship by loving them, nurturing them, and letting them see that they can come to you any time and talk to you about anything.

I learned this at an early age with Sarah. When she was about 13 years old she came to me one day and said, "Mother, sometimes I wish you wouldn't preach to me. Sometimes I wish you'd just listen. Sometimes I wish you wouldn't even give me your opinion. I'd just like for you to listen."

"Sarah," I assured her, "I *can* listen."

After that, she would come to me to tell me about a boy or about something that happened at school or a teacher who wasn't fair. She would go on and on and tell me everything, and I just listened. Then she'd ask me what I thought, and I got to tell her.

Sometimes she'd go on and on, and finally I'd ask if she wanted my opinion and she'd say yes! Most of the time children, especially teenagers, don't want our uninvited viewpoints. It's much better at that age if we wait for them to ask for an opinion. Try it sometime. Go a whole day or a whole week without volunteering your opinion even once. Your teenager will be frantic. They will start begging for your opinion. If they *ask* for it, they receive it well.

If you can learn to listen and not be shocked and not preach at them all the time (they probably know everything you're going to say anyway), then you will have more influence over them in the long run. Sometimes Sarah would come home late, and I'd be half asleep and she'd say, "Get up. I have to talk to you." Even now that she's an adult, she'll call sometimes and say, "I just want you to listen." Sometimes I'll ask if she wants an opinion and she'll reply "Nope, I don't want an opinion." When that happens, I keep my opinion to myself.

The Seeds of Love

Love creates love. Did God first love us, or were we born automatically loving God? He loved us first, and that love drew us to Him. It is His love that keeps us close to Him. If you love your children, you will draw them closer to you. If you hate your children, you will teach them to be haters. Using cruel words with your children will teach them to be cruel. By loving your children, you teach them how to love.

We all want loving relationships more than anything. Isn't that true? You're going to have to spend *quantity* time with your children if you want *quality* results. What you put into them is what you're going to get out of them. If you put nothing in except screaming, you are going to get screaming children!

We can't show God's love to our children until we experience God's love ourselves. It all starts when you receive the greatest love-gift that God has to give: His Son. When God gave Jesus Christ, He gave Him so that He could have a relationship with us. God didn't just give us Jesus to save us from hell or sin, He gave Him to us so that we could have a relationship with Him. Only our loving heavenly Father loved us so much that he would send His Son to die for us. That means that God loves us—He loves *you*—as much as He loves Jesus. That is an overwhelming thought, but it's the truth. He demonstrated it. He didn't just say it, He did it.

Chapter Six
Hope for Less-Than-Perfect Parents

Children don't come ready made. Just like making arrows, you clip this off, you shave that off, you try to shape some things. Sometimes you pull your hair, pray some more, and then get back to work. As they get older, you have different things to do. Eventually, there comes a time when you have to let that arrow go, and trust God that it will hit the mark. Don't give up. The only way you can fail is to quit. Just keep believing. When all else fails, pray!

Parenting is the most challenging job we are given, and it can be a rewarding job when everything turns out right. I don't want this book to discourage you in any way. Perhaps you are thinking, "If I had been different, if I had been a better, more godly parent, then my children would have turned out better. If I had done a better job, my children would be happier, more successful, and more spiritual." Let's get rid of those guilty thoughts right now, because guilt does not come from God.

One time, I was really down on myself as a parent. I said, "God, I have messed up this job you gave me. I've made so many mistakes with my children." I went through the whole list of all the things I wished I had done differently.

God replied, "Marilyn, I am the Father of Adam and Eve. Was I a good father?"

"Dear God, you cannot make mistakes," I answered. "Of course you were a good Father. You were a *perfect* Father!"

"Did Adam and Eve sin?" He asked.

"Yes, Father, they sinned."

Then God asked me, "Whose fault was it that they sinned? Was it My fault? Or was it their fault?"

Suddenly, I realized that even the children of the *only perfect Father* were sinners, too!

God continued with me. "I was the Father of Israel. Did Israel rebel?"

They rebelled over and over again

"Was that because I was a bad Father?" God asked, "or was it because they made their own choices?"

Children Make Choices, Too

We all try to do things that are good and right for our children, but we must always remember that our children make their own choices, too. Some of the things that they are going to do are not your fault, so get that monkey off your back. Put the monkey of guilt back on the devil, and trust God to take care of the places where you botched things. God knew you wouldn't be a perfect parent, but He is always there to help you. He will be there to help us improve as parents, and He will be there when we just can't do any more. Let the anointing of God touch and encourage you. Allow the Spirit to change you, make you a greater blessing, and give you hope for your children. The real hope for our children is not in the natural; it is not in what we see, feel, hear or say. The real hope for our children is in the supernatural: the anointing of the Holy Spirit.

There are many people in the Bible who went astray. Lot had two daughters who chose incest! David's family weren't all perfect. One of his sons was a rapist and another one was a murderer! Even so, God loved David very much, and David had some great successes with other children, and with his grandchildren and great-grandchildren. One of David's sons became the richest and most powerful king of Israel. Remember, Jesus came out of David's genealogy. God can bring forth good children out of you, even if you are not a perfect parent. All He asks is that you believe

Him, and trust Him for what you can't do, and for what you didn't do.

Monkey Business

If your children are young adults or middle-aged adults you may be thinking, "I did my best, but I can't interfere now. They won't listen to me. They think they are *my* parent." At that age, they want to tell you what to wear, what to eat, where to go. Sarah was lecturing me because she thought I was traveling too much. I said to her, "That's none of your business. You are married; you have your business; I have my business." She answered, "Mother, you will always be my business."

Sometimes, even our grown children can get into monkey business. When David had just become the king of 12 tribes, God said to him, "David, I'm going to make your house sure and secure. I'm going to build you a house that will never end. The throne of David will never end. The Messiah is going to come from your house."

Imagine what that meant to David! Now, look at David later in his life. David's son, Amnon, raped his own half sister. Another son, Absalom, killed Amnon and then stole the throne from David. Absalom even plotted to kill his own father.

David must have wondered how God would build his house, with sons like these! Sometimes we parents look at our children and say, "Dear God, you said raise a child in the way he should go and when he is old he won't depart from it, but my kids seem to depart from the Word every day." At times like these, it's important to remember that David's house didn't end. David's son Solomon was the richest, most powerful king Israel had ever seen. Solomon had a son, and those sons kept coming, until we got Jesus. God came through in spite of the bad choice that David's children made. David didn't do everything right, but the house of David is still standing.

Some of you may be thinking, "Well, this is a little late. Mine are grown." I want to encourage you that things you put in your children early do come up in their adulthood. Our son was at our house recently for his birthday, and he came to me.

"Mother," he told me, "I have a friend that I work with who is having a hard time following God. He really knows the Lord and has had a good walk with Him, but he says he just feels cold inside. He just keeps telling me this, and says, 'What would you do?' What should I tell him to do?"

75

I could hardly believe my son was asking me this. It's always such a surprise when our adult children ask for our advice! "Well, what did we teach you to do?" I questioned.

He went through all the things that we had taught him! We tried not to act too amazed! It is so encouraging that when we put that light inside them, it doesn't return void. Train up a child, create a desire in them, and when they are old, they will not depart from it.

Then my son gave us another surprise. He said, "Mother, the other day I met a friend that I went to school with. I asked him what he was doing and he said he had graduated from college and then got into computer programming, doing really well—but he also got into alcohol and drugs and his life went down the drain. Then, five years ago, he met Jesus Christ, and Jesus has totally changed his life!"

Is that God setting things up? If they won't hear quietly and quickly, God has ways of getting His still, small voice through all kinds of people to them. Right?

A Father's Prayers Are Answered

Don't ever despair! You are *not* a rotten parent. Just keep yourself immersed in the Word. What you can't say to them after they become young adults, you can *pray* into them. David did. Let's examine how he did it.

At the end of Psalms 72, David wrote *"The prayers of David the son of Jesse are ended"* (Psalms 72:20). Of all the prayers that David prayed, his very last prayers were for his son, Solomon, who was now king of Israel. Psalms 72 contains those final prayers of David. It is amazing to see what those prayers accomplished. For proof that God answers the prayers of parents, just look at what came true for Solomon.

In the first two verses of Psalms 72, David prayed:

"Give the king thy judgments, oh God, and thy righteousness, unto the king's son. He shall judge thy people with righteousness, and thy poor with judgment."

That prayer was fulfilled in Solomon in magnificent ways. If ever a man knew how to judge with the wisdom of God, it was Solomon. He was famous for his wisdom, and people came from all over the world to hear his righteous judgments.

In verse 7, David prayed: *"In his days shall the righteous flourish; and abundance of peace so long as the moon endureth."*

How wondrous to realize that there never was a battle in Solomon's reign! The word

Solomon means "peace," and there was total peace in Solomon's reign. Why? Because his father prayed these things into Solomon's life; they came to pass after the father was dead.

David kept right on praying for Solomon. In verse 10, he had this vision of Solomon's reign, *"The kings of Tarshish and of the isles shall bring presents: the kings of Sheba and Seba shall offer gifts,"* and in verse 15, he said, *"And he shall live and to him shall be given of the gold of Sheba: . . . and daily shall he be praised."* Long after David died, the queen of Sheba arrived with camel-loads of gold! The prayers of a parent can be so powerful!

That's not the end of it. Look at verse 17: *His name shall endure for ever: his name shall be continued as long as the sun: and men shall be blessed in him: all nations shall call him blessed.*

Did this one come true? Consider this. If you went out on the street today and walked up to the first person you met, and asked, "Have you ever heard of Solomon?" that person would probably say, "Yea, he's some wise guy." To this day, thousands of years later, Solomon is still known for his great wealth and his great wisdom. So his name has endured; it has continued.

Are men blessed in Solomon? Proverbs may

be one of the most quoted books in the Bible. They contain such great instruction, that even unbelievers quote them and are blessed by them! The author of much of this great book, beloved by everyone, was Solomon. Proverbs was not the only book he wrote. He wrote Song of Solomon and Ecclesiastes, too. Three "wisdom books" were written by the man whose father said, "His name will never end."

Solomon was a wise king who never had a war, enjoying peace throughout his reign. He is known to this day for his wisdom. Who prayed all this in? David did, long before it all came to pass. What you can't *pour* into them, you can *pray* into them. Parents can pray things into their kids that will keep going after they're gone and will bless people way down the line.

Prayer takes over where the natural stops and takes our children into the supernatural. Don't just look at what you see. Look up and see what He can do! When we pray the Word for our children, it cannot return void. Bow your head now, and pray this prayer for your children:

Father, I thank You that Your Word said that the seed of the righteous shall be delivered. That's Your promise, and I claim that promise for my household. The devil can't have my children. The devil is defeated, in Jesus' name. Satan, you have lost; you don't get my children; you don't get my grandchildren. These children are the seed of the righteous, and I give them into the love of the Father.

I am drawing a blood line around my self, my family, and my children. The devil cannot cross the bloodline. The blood overcomes him. The blood speaks to You, Father, and says, "Mercy, mercy, mercy" over my house, and over my loved ones, in Jesus' name.

Through Your power, my children will fulfill the destinies for which You made them. Thank You for being there when I have failed, when I have not been a perfect parent. I praise You for what You have done and will do, for my children, because You love them even more than I do.

Thank you, Father, that my seed will be mighty upon the earth. My seed will win souls and do mighty things in the name of Jesus. My seed will not just make it to heaven, they will bring many others in Jesus' name! Amen!

Chapter Seven
Creating Your Own Family Covenant

In this fast-paced society, we see many people, even Christians, who seem to go through life with no measurable goals. Ask today's high schoolers what their plans are after graduation, and you often receive a shrug of the shoulders and a mumbled, "I dunno. Guess I'll just hang out and get a job." There are a lot of people who don't know who they are, much less where they are going!

As Christian believers, it is important for us to have goals toward which we aim our faith, energies, and resources. The Word of God is filled with examples of God giving vision to His people. Abraham had clear direction from God to move from his homeland to a land far away. Moses' goal was to take the Hebrew children to the Promised Land. God made man to function best with clearly articulated goals, ***"Where there is no vision, the people perish: . . . "*** (Proverbs 29:18).

The word *perish* in the Hebrew means "to be loosened of restraint." Without a vision, people have no standard to live by, nothing to keep them from chaos.

Families, like individuals, need a clear understanding or vision of who they are and where they are headed as a unit. Parents and children both need a definite awareness of their *identity* and *destiny* as a family. One of the best ways to accomplish this corporate family vision is with a family covenant.

A family covenant is a written agreement made by each member of the family that gives a clear vision of what the family stands for and lives by: the values, spiritual principles, interests, and goals that define it and make it special. The family covenant serves as a target to help the family stay on track in fulfilling its God-given purpose and calling. Life may throw your family some curves, but a family covenant (and commitment to it) will anchor your family through rough water.

Define Your Family

The first step in creating a family covenant is to determine your distinct identity *as a family*. This is not a project for the parents only; it should include each family member. If your children take an active role in building the covenant, they will be more eager to follow it as they grow. They will feel as though they have "ownership" of it, so they will tend to give it authority in their lives.

Of course, the most important member of your family covenant should be your heavenly Father. He is an intimate member of your family and cares more about your family's success than anyone else.

When you are ready to begin creating your family covenant, depending on the personality and ages of your family members, it is good to get everyone together for several weekly discussion sessions. Make them as relaxed and fun as possible. If your children are small, keep the sessions very short. Consider holding your discussion in the backyard over ice cream sundaes or while roasting marshmallows over a campfire. Have one person write down *all* the suggestions, ideas, and concerns. At later gatherings, you will refine the list until you all agree on the final relevant points. Don't neglect to pray before each meeting to invite God to join as part of the family.

Start your discussions with specific ground rules:

1. Everyone in the family is important and everyone's ideas are important, therefore, encourage everyone to listen to each other with respect. (Remember, parents, the more

involved your kids are, the more they will commit to the end result.)

2. When someone gives an opinion or idea, restate it back to them to indicate that you understand it correctly. Good communication is extremely important in families, and this is an excellent time to practice those skills as a family.

3. Write down every idea. Whether you have one person acting as the secretary with a notepad or you use colored markers on pasteboard, it is vital to record *every* idea.

The best way to begin defining your family is to give each person a list of questions. If you have children who are deep thinkers, you might pass out the questions one week and ask for their response the next.

Here is a list of suggested questions:

- ✔ What is the purpose of our family?
- ✔ What are the principles and guidelines most important to this family?
- ✔ What kind of home would you like to invite your friends to?
- ✔ What kind of feelings do you want to have in this family?
- ✔ What are our responsibilities as family members?
- ✔ How do we want to treat each other;

what kind of relationships do we want
to have with each other?

✔ What about our family embarrasses
you and why?

These are meaningful questions that
should not be handled superficially. Small
children may say they want a family that
laughs and plays together, while older ones
may feel a need for their privacy to be
respected. As you spend time working through
these issues, you may end up setting aside
one night a week to watch silly movies
together or defining exactly what that teen's
"privacy" looks like.

There are a lot of different ways to
streamline your initial lists into a coherent,
concise statement of purpose and principles.
Discussion is important, regardless of your
elimination process. Some families vote on
each item, others ask each member to write
down their top five values and then eliminate
them one at a time until only one remains.

Creating a family covenant is an
opportunity for God to do a supernatural work
in your family. He will use it to give you, as
parents, a clearer, richer insight into your
children's hearts, while providing you an
occasion to examine your own hearts as well.
It is an opportunity for parents to really clarify

values and principles to their children's understanding. In short, there is no limit to what God can accomplish in this deeply spiritual, bonding activity.

One final thing to keep in mind is that you are not writing a formal, legal document; you are creating something that is a unique expression of your family. Maybe in your family, a certain word or phrase says it all or a specific object best defines your family. There is no right or wrong family covenant as long as it is a reflection of God's plan for your family and is a composite of each member's input.

Write the Vision

God is a big advocate of keeping the vision before your eyes. He gave the prophet, Habakkuk, a vision one time and wanted him to write it down, *"And the LORD answered me, and said, Write the vision, and make it plain upon tables, that he may run that readeth it"* (Habakkuk 2:2).

Once you have drafted your family covenant, write it down and keep it in a prominent place for everyone to see on a regular basis. If someone in the family does needlepoint, maybe they'd like to embroider and frame the family covenant. Whatever talents your family possesses, utilize them to create an attractive reminder to all involved, then place it where it can be easily seen.

As a family, look at it frequently and ask yourselves, "How are we measuring up? Are we living up to what we have decided to be and do?" Figure out from your answers if and where you are off-course. Then make course corrections as needed to attain your agreed-upon destination.

Three Hazards to Avoid

As you work with your family in developing your covenant, there are a few pitfalls that you will want to sidestep. Dodging these will promote family peace and success as you meet together to create your family covenant.

1. Don't proclaim it as a king does a new decree. In other words, don't be the "heavy" and use a statement you and your mate devise as an opportunity to "lay down the law" to your children. If your children are not part of the creative process, they will resent more rules. However, if they have been a part of the process, they will feel like the covenant represents them and they will be much more supportive.

2. Don't rush it. The more you allow the Holy Spirit to work with your family *as a family unit,* the more good results you will see. Never forget: **the process you go through is as important as the final result is in shaping the destiny of your family.** Listening to each family member and talking through rough spots is crucial to your family's well-being.

3. Once it is written, don't ignore it. Ask the Holy Spirit to help you put your covenant into practice in every area of your family's lives. Be alert to His voice telling you when you've missed it. As you stay tender-hearted about it and accountable to it, your family will follow your example.

Special Family Situations
Childless couples

If your family is just you and your spouse, you may want to plan a romantic weekend away or a series of dinner dates to formulate your covenant. Since you married someone who did not grow up in the same home with you, your spouse has some very basic different views and opinions of marriage and family. Creating a family covenant early in your marriage may help you avoid future problems as you work at defining terms and clarifying issues.

Review your marriage ceremony. You may get some good ideas from it, especially if you as a couple spent time composing it. Some good questions to ask yourselves are:

- What are the most important principles we want our marriage to exemplify?
- How do we serve God in the context of our marriage?
- How do we want to treat each other?
- How are we going to resolve conflicts?
- How are we going to handle our finances?

Where do we stand on:

- ✔ debt?
- ✔ in-law relationships?
- ✔ child training and discipline?
- ✔ family traditions and holidays?

- How do we develop God's gifts in our children?
- What traits did each of us learn in our childhood environment that we would like to change, and how do we expect to change them?

Use this time as you are creating your family covenant to explore each other's values and grow in greater understanding and appreciation of your mate. Allow the Holy Spirit to speak to your hearts as you work through this process.

Couples with grown children

If you and your mate have already raised your children, it is still not too late to make a family covenant. If your family is close-knit, you might want to involve your children and grandchildren, using many of the thought-provoking questions suggested earlier in this chapter.

If you and your spouse are making your own family covenant, here are some good questions to explore:

- What principles are most important to us in dealing with our children and grandchildren?
- What are the boundaries for our involvement in their lives?
- How can we encourage them to deal with their challenges and problems?
- What needs do they have that we can help meet?
- How do we handle the challenges of aging in the context of our spiritual values?

Blended families

If you have a blended family, you already realize that you have a lot of challenges to face. One of the things that may help older children in blended families buy into the family covenant concept is if you and your spouse first develop a covenant between yourselves. Once you have a solid covenant, the power of this agreement will help you provide the stability your teens so desperately need. In most cases, as you pray fervently and are consistent in your responses to them and each other, they will eventually recognize that you are the only really solid thing in their lives and they will begin to respond more positively. Be patient, knowing God is at work!

You may have to make a family covenant at first with those in the family who are willing to cooperate. It is important to set a compass for your blended family with as many as are willing.

Continue to unconditionally love the ones who are not as cooperative. God will work on their hearts as you follow Him steadfastly.

Scripture References
Put The Word to Work in Your Family

Once Every Month

Reinforce what your family stands for.
Proverbs 24:3,4
Through wisdom is an house builded; and by understanding it is established: And by knowledge shall the chambers be filled with all precious and pleasant riches.
See also: Proverbs 3:1, 4:8, 7:2, 15:32, & 20:11

Update house rules, adjust privileges and responsibilities.
Proverbs 5:7
Hear me now therefore, O ye children, and depart not from the words of my mouth.

Have a long heart-to-heart chat.
Proverbs 22:6
Train up a child in the way he should go: and when he is old, he will not depart from it.

Plan a fun-filled excursion.
Proverbs 13:22

Do some community service together. Organize, recycle, and give to the needy.
Proverbs 21:13
Whoso stoppeth his ears at the cry of the poor, he also shall cry himself, but shall not be heard.

Enjoy a family tradition.
Proverbs 13:22
A good man leaveth an inheritance to his children's children: and the wealth of the sinner is laid up for the just.

Once a week

Pursue a common interest or hobby with your kids.
Proverbs 15:30
The light of the eyes rejoiceth the heart: and a good report maketh the bones fat.

Think of a way to express admiration.
Proverbs 18:21
Death and life are in the power of the tongue:

and they that love it shall eat the fruit thereof.
**Arrange for some one-on-one time with your
child. Spend an evening with "just family."**
Proverbs 31:27
*She looketh well to the ways of her household,
and eateth not the bread of idleness.*

Give an allowance and teach saving.
Proverbs 13:11
*Wealth gotten by vanity shall be diminished:
but he that gathereth by labour shall increase.*

Make sure children complete chores.
Proverbs 10:4
*He becometh poor that dealeth with a slack
hand: but the hand of the diligent maketh rich.*

**Help your child perform an anonymous
good deed.**
Proverbs 21:21
*He that followeth after righteousness and mercy
findeth life, righteousness, and honour.*

Go on a date with your spouse.
Proverbs 5:18
*Let thy fountain be blessed: and rejoice with
the wife of thy youth.*

Review schoolwork.
Proverbs 16:20
He that handleth a matter wisely shall find good: and whoso trusteth in the LORD, happy is he.

Two to Three Times a Month

Take pictures. Review goals; reward when reached. Teach a life skill such as cooking or doing laundry.
Proverbs 12:24
The hand of the diligent shall bear rule: but the slothful shall be under tribute.

Ask how life is going—"How's school, friends, family?"
Proverbs 13:20
He that walketh with wise men shall be wise: but a companion of fools shall be destroyed.

Try a new recipe with your kids.
Proverbs 4:11
I have taught thee in the way of wisdom; I have led thee in right paths.

Visit a library.
Proverbs 12:1
Whoso loveth instruction loveth knowledge: but he that hateth reproof is brutish.
See also: Proverbs 15:20

Take time to rejuvenate yourself. Be spontaneous; don't overschedule.
Proverbs 8:14
Counsel is mine, and sound wisdom: I am understanding; I have strength.

Every Day

Say, "I love you." Read to your children. Kiss good night. Hug.
Proverbs 23:25
Thy father and thy mother shall be glad, and she that bare thee shall rejoice.

Forgive your kids.
Proverbs 10:18
He that hideth hatred with lying lips, and he that uttereth a slander, is a fool.

Forgive yourself.
Proverbs 4:23
Keep thy heart with all diligence; for out of it are the issues of life.

Help kids develop self-discipline (by cleaning their rooms, practicing piano, earning money, etc.).
Proverbs 14:15
The simple believeth every word: but the prudent man looketh well to his going.

Laugh about something.
Proverbs 15:15
All the days of the afflicted are evil: but he that is of a merry heart hath a continual feast.

Check kids' homework.
Proverbs 4:23
Keep thy heart with all diligence; for out of it are the issues of life.

Get sleep and exercise. Listen. Limit TV viewing.
Proverbs 27:12
A prudent man foreseeth the evil, and hideth himself; but the simple pass on, and are punished.

Make sure kids eat right. Keep children safe and healthy.

Proverbs 27:23

Be thou diligent to know the state of thy flocks, and look well to thy herds.

Teach kindness by example. Give children choices.

Proverbs 23:26

My son, give me thine heart, and let thine eyes observe my ways.

Good children bring joy.

Proverbs 10:1

The Proverbs of Solomon. A wise son maketh a glad father: but a foolish son is the heaviness of his mother.

See also: Proverbs 13:1 & 15:20.

Follow through.

Proverbs 10:5

He that gathereth in summer is a wise son: but he that sleepeth in harvest is a son that causeth shame.

Say, "Thank you."

Bibliography

Covey, Stephen R. *The 7 Habits of Highly Effective Families.* New York: Golden Books, 1997.

The Online Bible Thayer's Greek Lexicon and Brown Driver & Briggs' Hebrew Lexicon. Ontario: Woodside Bible Fellowship, 1993.

Receive Jesus Christ as Lord and Savior of Your Life.

The Bible says, *"That if thou shalt confess with thy mouth the Lord Jesus, and shalt believe in thine heart that God raised him from the dead, thou shalt be saved. For with the heart man believeth unto righteousness; and with the mouth confession is made unto salvation"* (Romans 10:9,10).

To receive Jesus Christ as Lord and Savior of your life, sincerely pray this prayer from your heart:

Dear Jesus,

I believe that You died for me and that You rose again on the third day. I confess to You that I am a sinner and that I need Your love and forgiveness. Come into my life, forgive my sins, and give me eternal life. I confess You now as my Lord. Thank You for my salvation!

Signed _____

Date _____

Write to us.
We will send you information to help you with your new life in Christ.

Marilyn Hickey Ministries ● P.O. Box 17340
Denver, CO 80217 ● (303) 770-0400

BOOKS BY MARILYN HICKEY

A Cry for Miracles ($7.95)
Acts of the Holy Spirit ($7.95)
Angels All Around ($7.95)
Armageddon ($4.95)
Ask Marilyn ($9.95)
Be Healed ($9.95)
Blessing Journal ($4.95)
Bible Encounter Classic Edition
  ($24.95)
Book of Revelation Comic Book (The)
  ($3.00)
Break the Generation Curse ($7.95)
Break the Generation Curse Part 2
  ($9.95)
Daily Devotional ($7.95)
Dear Marilyn ($7.95)
Devils, Demons, and Deliverance
  ($9.95)
Divorce Is Not the Answer ($7.95)
Especially for Today's Woman
  ($14.95)
Freedom From Bondages ($7.95)
Gift-Wrapped Fruit ($2.95)
God's Covenant for Your Family
  ($7.95)

God's Rx for a Hurting Heart ($4.95)
Hebrew Honey ($14.95)
How to Be a Mature Christian ($7.95)
Know Your Ministry ($4.95)
Maximize Your Day . . . God's Way
  ($7.95)
Names of God (The) ($7.95)
Nehemiah—Rebuilding the Broken
  Places in Your Life ($7.95)
No. 1 Key to Success—Meditation
  (The) ($4.95)
Proverbs Classic Library Edition
  ($24.95)
Release the Power of the Blood
  Covenant ($4.95)
Satan-Proof Your Home ($7.95)
Save the Family Promise Book
  ($14.95)
Signs in the Heavens ($7.95)
What Every Person Wants to
  Know About Prayer ($4.95)
When Only a Miracle Will Do ($4.95)
Your Miracle Source ($4.95)
Your Total Health Handbook—
  Body • Soul • Spirit ($9.95)

MINI-BOOKS: $1⁰⁰ each
by Marilyn Hickey

Beat Tension
Bold Men Win
Bulldog Faith
Change Your Life
Children Who Hit the Mark
Conquering Setbacks
Don't Park Here
Experience Long Life
Fasting and Prayer
God's Benefit: Healing
God's Seven Keys to Make
  You Rich
Hold On to Your Dream
How to Become More Than
  a Conqueror
How to Win Friends

I Can Be Born Again and Spirit Filled
I Can Dare to Be an Achiever
Keys to Healing Rejection
Power of Forgiveness (The)
Power of the Blood (The)
Receiving Resurrection Power
Renew Your Mind
Solving Life's Problems
Speak the Word
Standing in the Gap
Story of Esther (The)
Tithes • Offerings • Alms • God's
  Plan for Blessing You
Turning Point
Winning Over Weight
Women of the Word

Prices are in U.S. dollars. If ordering in foreign currency, calculate the current exchange rate.

For Your Information
Free Monthly Magazine

☐ Please send me your free monthly magazine,
OUTPOURING (including daily
devotionals, timely articles, and ministry
updates)!

Tapes and Books

☐ Please send me Marilyn's latest product
catalog.

Mr. & Mrs.
Mr.
Miss
Name Mrs. _____   Please print.

Address _____

City _____

State _____ Zip _____

Phone (H) ( ) _____

(W) ( ) _____

Mail to:
Marilyn Hickey Ministries
P.O. Box 17340
Denver, CO 80217
(303) 770-0400

Marilyn Hickey Ministries

Marilyn was a public school teacher when she met Wallace Hickey. After their marriage, Wally was called to the ministry and Marilyn began teaching home Bible studies.

The vision of Marilyn Hickey Ministries is to "cover the earth with the Word" (Isaiah 11:9). For more than 30 years Marilyn Hickey has dedicated herself to an anointed, unique, and distinguished ministry of reaching out to people—from all walks of life—who are hungry for God's Word and all that He has for them. Millions have witnessed and acclaimed the positive, personal impact she brings through fresh revelation knowledge that God has given her through His Word.

Marilyn has been the invited guest of government leaders and heads of state from many nations of the world. She is considered by many to be one of today's greatest ambassadors of God's Good News to this dark and hurting generation.

The more Marilyn follows God's will for her life, the more God uses her to bring refreshing, renewal, and revival to the Body of Christ throughout the world. As His obedient servant, Marilyn desires to follow Him all the days of her life.

Marilyn and Wally adopted their son Michael; through a fulfilled prophecy they had their daughter Sarah, who with her husband Reece, is now part of the ministry.

Marilyn taught at Denver's "Happy Church" and hosted ministry conferences with husband Wally.

Marilyn started on radio, but soon realized how many more people she could reach by going on television "Today With Marilyn" Bible teaching program is broadcast weekdays on TBN, BET, and several independent stations. The program is also seen overseas by millions through Christian Network TV in South Africa, in Australia on Network 10, and in more than 80 other countries worldwide.

In Venezuela with first lady Mrs. Perez

Marilyn has been the invited guest of government leaders and heads of state from many nations of the world.

In Egypt with Mrs. Anwar Sadat

The ministry has expanded to its present headquarters located in Greenwood Village, Colorado.

Marilyn Hickey's Prayer Center handles calls from all over the U.S.— ministering to those who need agreement in prayer.

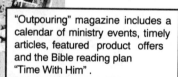

"Outpouring" magazine includes a calendar of ministry events, timely articles, featured product offers and the Bible reading plan "Time With Him".

More than 1,500 ministry products help people in all areas of their life.

Through Word to the World College, Marilyn is helping to equip men and women to take the gospel around the world.

Marilyn speaks in Korea at Dr. Cho's church and is on the board of directors.

God has opened doors for the supplying of Bibles to many foreign lands—China, Israel, Poland, Ethiopia, Russia, Romania, and Ukraine, just to name a few.

Marilyn and Sarah have a heart for China and for ministering overseas.

Food, Bibles, and water wells have been supplied to many countries, such as Haiti, the Philippines, Ethiopia, Honduras, India and El Salvador.

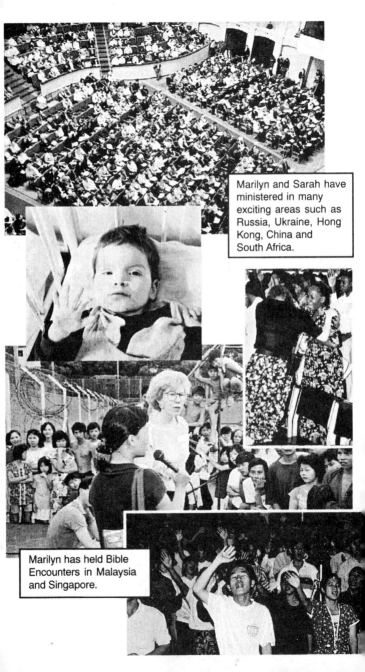

Marilyn and Sarah have ministered in many exciting areas such as Russia, Ukraine, Hong Kong, China and South Africa.

Marilyn has held Bible Encounters in Malaysia and Singapore.

Ministry trips and cruises to places such as Indonesia, Russia, Greece, Ukraine, Turkey, and Israel offer short-term missions' opportunities to travel with Marilyn.

Overseas offices have recently been set up in the United Kingdom, Australia, and South Africa. Marilyn also hosts yearly meetings, crusades, and missions' projects in those countries.

Marilyn ministers to and teaches thousands at Encounters and Miracle Healing Crusades overseas, as well as in the U.S.

Crowds of up to 200,000 attended the open-air crusade in Bangalore, India.

In Islamabad, Pakistan, Marilyn held Ministry Training Schools and crusades where crowds grew nightly to approximately 70,000 by closing night.

Eritrea and Sudan—Ministry Training Schools, nightly crusades and Madagascar crusade with Sarah and Marilyn ministering